D1560223

MODIFYING CLASSROOM BEHAVIOR

A MANUAL OF PROCEDURE FOR CLASSROOM TEACHERS

by

Nancy K. Buckley

Psychologist, Spanish Peaks Mental Health Center, Pueblo, Colorado

Hill M. Walker

Department of Special Education, University of Oregon, Eugene, Oregon

RESEARCH PRESS

2612 NORTH MATTIS AVE. · CHAMPAIGN, ILLINOIS 61820

Library of Congress Catalog Card Number: 72-075092

ISBN 0-87822-008-9

Introduction

Teaching children in a classroom today probably demands more diversified skills than ever before. A variety of reasons could be given for this such as the increased emphasis on, and need for, education; the more complex technology with its demands on the teacher to master a variety of subject knowledge; and children who are healthier, stronger, and beginning to learn at an earlier age than ever before. Another important reason for new teacher skills is that we are now, as educators and psychologists, in a better position to study how children learn both academically and socially. This discovery has its most important implications for classroom discipline and control both of the group as a whole and individuals within the group.

Most behaviors are learned through the environment in which a child finds himself. While in the classroom, children are learning many ways to misbehave as well as behave. The classroom provides a setting in which a child *can* learn adaptive behavior and unlearn maladaptive behavior.

In the same way that the child learns through his environment, the teacher's behavior is shaped by the reactions of the children and colleagues of the teacher. Techniques used in the classroom are a result of the reinforcement a teacher receives. The children teach the teachers how to act, and our actions do not always reflect the most appropriate method(s).

Psychologists and educators are looking closely at *how* behavior is learned in an effort to strengthen behaviors in children which help them to develop into productive young citizens. Many of the techniques used for this purpose are not new. There may be some you have used in your classroom. The novelty results from approaching the problem in a systematic and consistent manner. We can look at the behavior and the setting and determine what techniques to use, why to use them, and whether we are being successful in changing the behavior.

The principles of behavior modification are derived from experimental work which studies the relationship between the environment and an individual's overt behavior. Ullmann & Krasner (1966) state that

> The working behavior therapist is likely to ask three questions: (a) what behavior is maladaptive, that is, what subject behaviors should be increased or decreased; (b) what environmental contingencies currently support the subject's behavior (either to maintain his undesirable behavior or to reduce the likelihood of his performing a more adaptive response), and (c) what environmental changes, usually reinforcing stimuli, may be manipulated to alter the subject's behavior.

The following programmed lessons are designed to explain the theory and techniques of classroom behavior modification.

N. K. B.
H. M. W.

To the Reader:

This book has been written for use by teacher trainees and practicing teachers. The attempt has been to keep the book as brief and nontechnical in its terminology and concepts as possible without omitting relevant information. For those students and teachers interested in learning more about the procedures and applications of behavior modification, the authors have included a list of suggested reading in the appendix.

In developing the format of the text, the authors chose to incorporate both prose and programmed items to form a semiprogrammed content.* This design was selected to enhance reader interest and at the same time make use of the advantages of programmed instruction. Programmed instruction has been shown effective in learning material because it incorporates: (a) immediate feedback, (b) small steps, (c) active responding, and (d) self-pacing.

The chapters have been divided into sets. Each set represents a different concept important to the chapter focus. Each set begins with a prose section designed to present all new materials.

The programmed items were selected to give feedback to the reader regarding understanding of the prose material. In addition, the programmed items, or frames, incorporate classroom application of the concepts.

It is important that the reader respond actively to each of the items. The response areas are large enough for responses to be written directly into the text. A folded paper should be used to conceal the answers at the bottom of the page. Once a response has been made, the reader moves the paper far enough to check his answer with that of the text. Learning is much more effective if the reader responds prior to checking the answer. If any questions are not answered correctly, one should reread the preceding prose section before continuing.

---

*Smith, W. I. and Moore, J. W. *Conditioning and instrumental learning.* New York: McGraw-Hill, 1966.

Each of the programmed items requires one of the following responses:

---

1. Fill-in missing word, e.g., "When the reader actually writes the answer down he is using the principle of active _____."

2. Circle the correct response of two choices, e.g., "If each step the student takes is small, he (is, is not) likely to make errors."

3. Check the appropriate answer or answers from several possible choices, e.g., "Which of the following are principles of programmed instruction?"
    _____a. Immediate confirmation.
    _____b. Active responding.
    _____c. Hidden "trick" questions.
    _____d. Self-pacing.
    _____e. Rapid skimming.

Many of the sets contain exhibits. These exhibits are excerpts from actual research done in the field of behavior modification. The exhibits were selected to illustrate and support the various concepts in the book as well as to serve as stimuli to the reader for further study in the field.

Since the excerpts are in most cases direct quotes from journals, the language is more technical than that of the book. However, complete understanding of the exhibits is not necessary for mastery of the text.

A second revision of the program was used as a basic text in a university extension class for regular, elementary teachers. The class was entitled *Coping With Classroom Behavior* and dealt with applications of operant techniques, behavior modification, and precision teaching in the regular classroom setting. There were twenty teachers in the class and each completed all frames in the program. An item analysis of the results yielded an average of 90% correct on the first trial for the total frames. These data were used as a basis for the third revision in the elimination and reworking of items.

---

1. responding   2. is not   3. a, b, d

Table of Contents

Part 1: Basic Principles

Section A: How Behaviors Are Learned

SET 1: *Acquisition of Behavior*

The behaviors a person emits throughout his lifetime are learned through the environment in which he finds himself. We act in a manner which we feel is most appropriate to (will help us get along best in) that environment. From childhood parents, teachers, peers and even strangers provide cues and reinforcement for responses to the environment. Even the objects of physiological drives such as the types of food we eat, the people we find attractive and so forth, are learned from our associates and society in general.

Not only are desirable behaviors a function of the environment but deviant behaviors as well. The same principles apply to the production and elimination of deviant or undesirable behavior that apply to production and elimination of desirable behavior. Obviously a teacher would not knowingly encourage a child to talk out, hit children, and exhibit other behaviors maladaptive to the classroom setting. Nevertheless, such behaviors are produced and maintained by some part of the child's environment which in this case may be teacher or peers.

When undesirable behaviors are present we can assume they are a result of (a) the correct (adaptive) behavior has never been learned, and/or (b) an incorrect (maladaptive) behavior has been learned which conflicts with the performance of the correct behavior. The difference between these two processes has important implications for the treatment strategies employed. For example, before punishing a maladaptive response a teacher should be aware of whether an alternative adaptive response is in the child's repertoire. If the response is not it should be taught prior to, or at the same time as eliminating the maladaptive response.

1. By environment is meant:
   _____a. the geographical climate in which we live.
   _____b. the physical surroundings only, such as city vs. country.
   _____c. the surroundings of a person including people, institutions and norms.

2. Most of the things we generally consider part of a person's "personality" are (learned, not learned) from the environment.

3. A new child is admitted to the classroom. If he does not raise his hand when responding we must assume:
   _____a. he has not learned to raise his hand.
   _____b. an incorrect behavior, talking out, has been learned.
   _____c. either a or b, or both.

4. Upon further investigation we find that the child has been ill and tutored at home for three years prior to entering this class. Thus which of the responses in 3, above, might we assume to be correct? a

5. Suppose instead that the child has been going to public school for four years but still shouts out answers. We notice the teacher acknowledges his answers. Thus we can assume, to be correct, which of the choices in #3? b

---

1. c

2. learned

3. c

4. a

5. b

4

6. At a parent conference you mention to Ricky's mother that he loses his temper frequently. She responds by saying, "I know but what can I do, he gets that from his father. His side of the family is known for their tempers—they're Irish you know." From this information you know:

    _____a. that Ricky has inherited his temper from his parent.

    _____b. that Ricky may have *learned* to act the way he does from the actions of a parent.

7. The information given by the mother is of little help in solving Ricky's problem. Such statements appear to be attempts at excusing the behavior rather than preventing it. We can assume that Ricky and his father "lose" their tempers not because of inherited traits but because in the past temper losses have been _____. Or, Ricky and his father have not learned an appropriate alternative _____ or both.

---

6. b

7. learned

    response (behavior)

The reason we continue to emit behaviors over time is because of the reinforcers available for such behaviors. Reinforcer (reinforcing stimulus) is defined as "an event which changes subsequent behavior when it follows behavior in time." (Morse, in Honig, 1966.) The reinforcer is called a positive reinforcer when its *presentation* increases the likelihood of a response.

Both adaptive and maladaptive behaviors are learned because of the reinforcers available for such behavior. When a behavior is reinforced the chance (probability) of that behavior occurring again is increased. However, if the behavior is not reinforced the behavior tends to stop occurring or "drop out" of the subject's response repertoire.

EXHIBIT 1

To illustrate the principle that reinforcement alone can increase a behavior and its withdrawal can decrease that same behavior, researchers often use a "reversal of contingencies" design. With this procedure the behavior under study is measured, an experimental variable is applied (in this case reinforcement) and any change is noted. If a change in behavior occurs (see Reinf.$_1$) the experimental variable (reinforcement) is withdrawn or altered (see Reversal). If the change was due to the reinforcement, the measured behavior should be reduced to pre-experimental (baseline) level.

In a study by Hall, Lund, and Jackson (1968) the effects of teacher attention on study behavior were measured. With one first-grade and five third-grade children—described as having disruptive or dawdling behavior—the experimenters were able to increase study behavior with teacher attention for study behavior and ignoring non-study behaviors. During a reversal of contingencies, attention was given only after periods of non-study behavior. This reversal produced low rates of study behavior.

The following graph represents the study behavior for one subject in the Hall, Lund, and Jackson study.

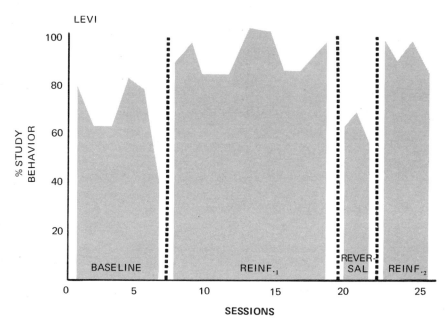

Fig. 1 ". . . study occurred in approximately 88% of the intervals of Reinforcement and at no time went below that of the highest baseline rate. A brief reversal produced a marked decrease in study to a mean rate of 60%. However, when reinforcement for study was reinstated study again rose to above baseline rate (p. 10)."

8. By making reinforcement available we increase the likelihood that the child will practice what we teach him. A common word for a positive _____ is reward.

9. A child who is usually noisy in the hall has been very quiet and asks to carry the balls. Letting him carry the balls can serve as a _____ for walking quietly in the hall.

8. reinforcer   9. reinforcer (or) reward

10. When a child does well on a quiz he can be praised. Praise serves as a reinforcer for good grades and tends to (increase, decrease) the chances of another good paper.

11. In discussion periods one child waves his hand and impatiently says "I know, I know," when the teacher poses a question to the class. If the teacher calls on this child she is reinforcing _____ _____ and _____ _____.

12. Thus we can expect hand waving and verbal outbursts to (increase, decrease) for this child.

13. When a baby emits language sound approximations it brings smiles and caresses from adults present. We can assume that the caresses and attention are desirable or _____ ing to the child. Thus the behavior which increased adult attention, *sound production*, will be more likely to occur again.

14. If no one pays attention to the sound approximations, i.e., they are not reinforced, they will tend to _____ _____.

---

10. increase

11. hand waving

    verbal outbursts

12. increase

13. *reinforc*ing (or) *reward*ing

14. drop out (or) stop occurring

It is important to look at how new behaviors are learned, i.e., behaviors which have never been displayed before by the child. One method for learning new behaviors is by observation and imitation. A child sees or hears someone perform a particular behavior and he may copy or imitate that behavior. This type of imitative behavior is referred to as *modeling.* We see another person, the model, do something and we copy it. Modeling is most likely to occur when the observer sees the model obtain some type of reinforcer for emitting the behavior. The observer receives vicarious reinforcement from the reinforcement administered to the model (Bandura and Walter, 1963a). There are a variety of theories of imitation (e.g., Humphrey, 1921; Allport, 1924; Miller and Dollard, 1941; Mowrer, 1960) which suggest various hypotheses for the emergence of novel responses. Experimental work (Bandura and Walters, 1963b), gives strong support to acquisition of both adaptive and maladaptive behavior through modeling.

Modeling is very obvious in the behaviors of young children. Most children learn to speak, ride bicycles, identify with their sex, and so forth, by imitating the actions of others.

Throughout life we are guided in our actions by film, verbal and actual models. The use of a model can be a constructive way to build up desirable behaviors in children.

EXHIBIT 2

"In a study designed to test for delayed imitation of deviant models in the absence of the models, Bandura, Ross, and Ross (1961) exposed one group of nursery-school children to aggressive adult models and a second group to models who displayed inhibited and nonaggressive behavior. Half of the children in each of these conditions observed models of the same sex as themselves, while the remaining children in each group were exposed to models of the opposite sex. For the aggressive-model group the model exhibited unusual forms of physical and verbal aggression toward a large inflated plastic doll. In contrast, the nonaggressive-model group observed an adult who sat very quietly, totally ignoring the doll and the instruments of aggression that had been placed in the room."

"The children who observed the aggressive models displayed a great number of precisely imitative aggressive responses, whereas such responses rarely occurred in either the nonaggressive-model group or the control group. Moreover, children in the nonaggressive-model group displayed the inhibited behavior characteristic of their model to a greater extent than did the control children. In addition, the results [Bandura, Ross, and Ross, 1963] indicated that film-mediated models are as effective as real-life models in transmitting deviant patterns of behavior (p. 61–61)."

---

15. When a teacher says, "Look how nicely Johnny sits in his chair," she is using Johnny as a model for the right way to _____.

16. A gangster hero on T.V. may serve as a film _____ for illegal behavior.

17. A well-mannered child who is the subject of a book read in class may be a verbal _____ for good student behavior.

    Based on what you have read thus far on reinforcement and modeling, consider the following hypothetical situations (#18–21).

    In Miss Brown's fourth grade class, Joe throws a "spitwad" at Bob in the front of the room.

18. Miss Brown is busy helping a youngster and does not notice, but many of the children notice and giggle and look at Joe. The likelihood of Bob returning a spitwad is (increased, decreased) after seeing Joe throw one.

---

15. sit in a chair.   17. model

16. model   18. increased

19. Miss Brown saw Joe throw the paper and made him stay in during recess. After observing this interaction Bob would be (more, less) likely to model the behavior of Joe, i.e., throwing spitwads.

20. After watching Joe throw the spitwad, Bob makes a spitwad and tosses it to Joe's desk. Miss Brown sees Bob's spitwad and sends him to the principal's office. In this case Bob did not receive reinforcement for modeling Joe's behavior. Therefore, the behavior is likely to _____ _____.

21. Bob returns a spitwad toward Joe which goes unnoticed except by Joe who giggles and again throws a piece of paper. If we assume that the attention from Joe is reinforcing we can expect Bob's spitwad throwing to (increase, decrease) in frequency.

22. Miss A., a student teacher in Mr. C.'s fifth grade class, has trouble getting the children to quiet down after art class. She notices Mr. C. set a 3-minute egg timer and the noise ends abruptly after this period. The reinforcer available to Mr. C. in this case is:
    _____a. knowing Miss A. is having trouble with discipline.
    _____b. the egg timer.
    _____c. the quiet classroom.

23. Mr. C.'s reinforcement is available to him directly. If a quiet classroom is reinforcing for Miss A. she can receive _____ reinforcement for the same quietness.

---

19. less

20. drop out (or) decrease

21. increase

22. c

23. vicarious

24. If Mr. C. is an effective model for Miss A., next time she wants a quiet classroom she will:

_____a. have Mr. C. quiet the classroom.

_____b. use an egg timer.

_____c. eliminate art class.

24. b

SET 4: *Shaping*

Another method of teaching behaviors in addition to modeling is the method of Successive Approximations (shaping) and chaining. If a behavior has never been exhibited by a child we cannot reinforce the behavior. Therefore, to teach some behaviors we must reward behaviors which are close to, or approximate the desired behaviors.

As the general response comes to be exhibited more frequently, we reward a step closer to the desired specific response. From this gradual refining of the reinforced response we get the name Successive Approximation.

An example of the method of Successive Approximation, or shaping, is the gradual progression in teaching a child to print. At first any approximation of the letter is accepted—i.e., *Ν* for "N." Gradually the child is required to make strokes more closely like an "N" before the teacher says "good." Reinforcing each small step toward a better "N" is using the method of Successive Approximation.

Not only must a child be taught how to make an "N" of the right shape but also the proper size and placement on a page. Putting all of these responses together to make one complete response is called chaining.

EXHIBIT 3

The following study illustrates not only the shaping procedure but also how aware the teacher must be of the contingencies operating when attempting to alter deviant behavior. Wolf, Risley and Mees (1964) in a now classical study used shaping to get a 3½ year old autistic boy to wear glasses.

"During the first several sessions a conditioned reinforcer was established by having the clicks of a toy noisemaker followed by Dicky's receiving small bites of candy or fruit. The click soon became a discriminative stimulus and after each click Dicky would go to the bowl where the reinforcers were placed.

"Since Dicky had worn the prescription glasses for a few seconds on at least one occasion and had not left them on, it was assumed that wearing them was not immediately reinforcing. The glasses might even have been mildly aversive, since they would drastically change all visual stimuli, as well as force the eyes into greater accommodation. Also, glasses with the full prescription had been paired in the past with attempts to physically force glasses-wearing.

"For these reasons we decided not to begin with the actual prescription glasses. Instead, several empty glasses frames were placed around the room and Dicky was reinforced for picking them up, holding them, and carrying them about. Slowly, by successive approximations, he was reinforced for bringing the frames closer to his eyes.

"The original plan was, after he was wearing the lenseless frames, to introduce plain glass and then prescription lenses in three steps of progressing severity. This was not the actual sequence of events, however, since our shaper met with considerable difficulty in getting Dicky to wear the glassless frames in the proper manner, i.e., with the ear pieces over instead of under the ears and the eye openings in line with the eyes. Furthermore, it was impossible to help place the frames correctly since Dicky became upset when anyone touched any part of his head.

"The slow progress was probably attributable to two factors. First, the attendant, although co-operative, was inexperienced and imprecise with the shaping procedure. Secondly, due to the reluctance of the ward staff to deprive the child of food we began with reinforcers such as candy and fruit. It soon became obvious, however, that, at least for this child, these were rather weak reinforcers.

"After the first two weeks we attempted to increase deprivational control by using breakfast as a shaping session, bites of breakfast now being dependent upon approximations to the wearing of glasses. Two weeks later we added to the glasses larger adult ear pieces and a 'roll bar' which would go over the top of his head and guide the ear pieces up and over the ears."

"After wearing the glasses was established in these sessions, it could be maintained with other, less manipulable reinforcers. For example, the attendant would tell Dicky, 'Put your glasses on and let's go for a walk.' Dicky was usually required to wear the glasses during meals, snacks, automobile rides, walks, outdoor play, etc. If he removed the glasses, the activity was terminated."

"At the time of Dicky's release from the hospital he had worn the glasses for more than 600 hrs. and was wearing them about 12 hrs. a day (p. 309–310)."

25. In using the methods of successive approximation and chaining to get a shy child to speak in front of the room, which of the following techniques would be used:

     ____a. require the child to give a three minute report each day in various topics of interest.

     ____b. begin at a level he can tolerate—e.g., reading in seat, reading to small group standing beside desk, reading to teacher only, reading in isolation, etc. After he feels comfortable at this step, gradually progress to the next logical step—e.g., moving closer to the front of the room, increasing the audience size.

     ____c. concentrate on his strengths. Work on encouraging the child to do the things he does well and don't require him to talk in front of the room.

26. In a gym class several of the boys cannot chin themselves for 15 seconds to pass the physical fitness test. Therefore, Mr. B. records the level which they can achieve—e.g., holding on to bar, pulling self halfway up, maintaining correct posture 1 second, etc. Over time he gradually *increases* the amount expected for each boy. He keeps an accurate record so as not to pass the child's physical limitations but at the same time continually increase achievement level by small amounts. This is an example of the method of _____ _____.

27. There are a variety of ways to correct "out of seat behavior" in a child who has trouble remaining in his seat. One of the most positive approaches for both teacher and child is to use successive approximations. Mrs. T. has recorded that Ron seldom stays in his seat for longer than five minutes at a time. Her goal is to get him to stay in his seat 15 minutes at a time without getting up, which is what most of her third grade pupils

---

25. b

26. successive approximation

average. Her first step should be to:

_____a. reinforce him each time he returns to his desk.

_____b. wait until he has been in his chair 4—5 minutes. Go to his desk and praise him or give him a token reinforcer.

_____c. tell him that other children can sit for 15 minutes and if he sits in his chair for 15 minutes he will get a point.

_____d. remind him each time he is out of his seat that he should sit quietly in order to get points.

28. When Ron has been able to sit for several five minute periods this is a sign to Mrs. T. to:

_____a. increase the time required to 10 minutes.

_____b. increase the time required to 15 minutes. (Her goal)

_____c. increase the time required to 6—7 minutes.

29. Assume that Mrs. T. increases the time required for in-seat behavior to 7 minutes. Ron sits approximately 5½ minutes then leaves his seat. This occurs several times in succession; each time he fails to stay for the full 7 minutes. This is a clue that the step was too _____ and she should drop back to 5½ minutes until he consistently succeeds at that level. She should then continue gradually increasing the time requirement until he can sit for 15 minutes at a time. (See intermittent reinforcement for maintenance.)

---

27. b. (A shorter time period might be necessary for another student but one must be careful not to reinforce the act of getting out of his seat.)

28. c

29. large

SUMMARY

1. The behaviors human beings exhibit are due to the interchange between the environment and the person.
2. Adaptive behaviors and maladaptive behaviors are learned in the same way.
3. Behaviors which are rewarded tend to be repeated.
4. New behaviors can be learned through one of two methods:
   a. modeling of someone or something in the environment.
   b. shaping and chaining of small responses to more closely approximate larger behaviors.

Section B: Why Behaviors Continue to Be Performed (Maintained)

SET 1: *Reasons for Studying Maintenance*

When presented with a behavior problem it often appears that the reason a child exhibits a certain behavior is because of some *one* thing that occurred in his past. As the following example illustrates this can often be misleading.

Betty, age five, throws tantrums when separated from her mother. The mother recalls that the first time she was aware of the behavior was after a long hospitalization when Betty was three. From this information we might quickly assume that Betty's temper tantrums at age five are caused by a traumatic separation earlier in her life. However, the child psychologist working with Betty's mother also discovers that each time Betty becomes upset her mother agrees not to leave, thus reinforcing the tantrums by giving Betty her way.

This example illustrates two important reasons for not looking for some original *cause*:

1. Determining how or why a child first performed a behavior is nearly impossible. We, of course, cannot directly observe the past history of an individual. Therefore, we must rely on reports from other persons or the individual himself. This type of reporting can be grossly inaccurate. In this case, we cannot be sure Betty had never had temper tantrums before the hospital separation.

2. The stimulus that maintains the behavior can be very different from the original stimulus for emitting the behavior.

In the illustration, the hospital separation is not causing the tantrums now; rather the reinforcement from mother remaining home strengthens and maintains the behavior.

It is helpful to look at a situation in terms of: (a) the event which occurred prior to the child's response (*the stimulus*); (b) the child's behavior (*the response*); and (c) what followed immediately after the child emitted the behavior (*the consequence*). The stimulus and the consequence are both changes in the child's environment. The response is a single instance of an observable and definable part of a child's behavior.

It is easier to see the relationship between a response and its consequence (a behavioral contingency) by charting the relationship schematically. One notational system which serves this purpose was developed by Mechner (1959). Basically, the schema shows the stimulus situation (S or S_1), the response (R) and the consequence (usually called S_2). A subscript number can be used to show a change in the situation or response, i.e., S_1, S_2 ... S_n or R_1, R_2 ... R_n. Thus the basic diagram would be:

$$\begin{bmatrix} S_1 \\ R \longrightarrow S_2 \end{bmatrix}$$

When using actual situations it is easier to simply write the event in subscript parentheses. Thus the contingency of leaving for lunch break might be diagrammed as follows:

$$\begin{bmatrix} S_{(Bell\ rings)} \\ R_{(T.\ excuses\ class)} \longrightarrow S_{(children\ leave\ room)} \end{bmatrix}$$

The bracket around the S_1 and R indicates that they occur simultaneously. That is, the situation must be present for the response to occur. The arrow indicates "leads to" or "produces."

In the case of Betty's tantrums, the analysis might be as follows:

(If)
$$\begin{bmatrix} S_1 & {}_{(Mother\ ready\ to\ leave\ B.)} \\ (then) & \\ & (leads\ to) \\ R & {}_{(B.\ throws\ tantrum)} \longrightarrow S_2\ {}_{(Mother\ stays\ home-\ reinforcer\ for\ tantrum)} \end{bmatrix}$$

1. As a classroom teacher you have a child who vomits when punished or forced to stay after school. You check his medical record and find no physiological reason for the vomiting. Upon calling his mother you learn that he does this frequently at

home when punished but the mother does not know what to do. You should:

    _____a. refer the child to a psychiatrist.

    _____b. work with the parents to determine how the vomiting started.

    _____c. look at your own behavior to see what *you* do when he vomits.

2. Brian, a fourth grader, has a "history" of fighting on the playground. This fighting has continued in the fourth grade. His teacher should:

    _____a. talk to his previous teachers to determine why he began to fight.

    _____b. refer him to the school counselor for group therapy.

    _____c. not allow him on the playground again.

    _____d. try to determine what is maintaining the behavior (the reinforcer) and eliminate it or change its reinforcing value.

3. Assume the following situation: A child is assigned 10 math problems (stimulus). He completes the problems (response), and the teacher says "very good." What is the consequence in this case?

$$\left[\begin{array}{l} S \text{ (Assignment)} \\ R \text{ (Working Problems)} \end{array}\right. \longrightarrow S^{R+} \quad a(?)$$

a._____

---

1. c

2. d

3.   a. Teacher praise ("very good")

4. A child is turned around talking to a peer. The teacher asks him to face the front of the room. He refuses, so is sent from the room. What are the missing parts of the contingency?

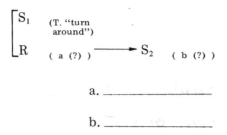

a. _____

b. _____

5. Brian is a large boy for his age but does poorly in P. E. activities. The teacher has tried to encourage him to participate but within the first five minutes he trips, pushes or in some other way upsets another student. When this occurs the teacher sends him off to play by himself.
Identify the contingencies that maintain this behavior.

$$\begin{bmatrix} S_1 & (\text{ a (?) }) \\ R & (\text{ b (?) }) \end{bmatrix} \longrightarrow S_2 \quad (\text{ c (?) })$$

a. _____

b. _____

c. _____

---

4. a. Refusal
    b. Sent from room

5. a. P. E. period
    b. upsets peers
    c. removal of Brian (escape from P. E.)

In understanding why behaviors continue to be emitted we can apply the general principle of reinforcement from Section A. When a person (child *or* teacher) is reinforced for exhibiting a certain behavior, that behavior is strengthened and will be more likely to be exhibited again in the future.

Positive reinforcement has an important function in the acquisition (learning) of new behaviors. It is equally important in maintaining behaviors that are already in a person's repertoire.

Each day we receive reinforcement in a variety of ways for our behavior. Three broad classes of reinforcers available are social reinforcers, token and tangible reinforcers, and intrinsic reinforcers.

By definition a reinforcer is an event which *changes* behavior. Therefore, any of the following may or may not be a reinforcer for any given person. They are only potential reinforcers.

As the term implies, social reinforcers are those that come from other persons in our environment. What we generally think of as reinforcing are praise, agreement, gestures of affection or approval. In the classroom a word or gesture of approval immediately following a behavior, if reinforcing, strengthens that behavior.

EXHIBIT 4

Becker, Madsen, Arnold and Thomas (1967) "worked in public schools with teachers who had problem children in their classes. Behaviors exhibited by the students were observed and the frequency of these behaviors was estimated for each child. Each teacher was taught to use praise, smiles, etc., to reinforce good behavior. The rate of appropriate classroom behaviors increased in most cases as soon as teacher approval and recognition were made contingent on such behavior (Thomas, et al., p. 35)."

An extension of this study by the same authors (Thomas, Becker, and Armstrong, 1968) used a class of 28 elementary students rated by the teacher as "good" "with an above-average distribution of ability and no 'bad' kids." Recordings were made on both teacher and child behaviors.

"The results demonstrated that approving teacher response served a positive reinforcing function in maintaining appropriate classroom behaviors. Disruptive behaviors increased each time approving teacher behavior was withdrawn. When the teacher's disapproving behaviors were tripled, increases appeared most markedly in the gross motor and noise-making categories of disruptive behavior. The findings emphasize again the important role of the teacher in producing, maintaining, and eliminating disruptive as well as prosocial classroom behavior (p. 35)."

Positive Reinforcement With Tokens

Token and tangible reinforcers cover an extremely broad class. Tangible reinforcers are things which can be eaten, looked at, smelled, touched, played with, and so forth. Commonly used reinforcers are candies, films, toys, trips, games and parties, or gold stars.

Tokens are objects which can be traded in on some tangible reinforcer. Such things as poker chips, check marks and colored papers can be used efficiently in a classroom. Other tangible reinforcers commonly used in the classroom are free time or special privileges.

Some reinforcers are originally neutral but acquire their potency from being paired with other reinforcers. These reinforcers are termed acquired or conditioned reinforcers. Money is a conditioned reinforcer because it is valuable not for its own properties but for what it can buy in primary reinforcers.

A wide variety of token and tangible reinforcers are available in our lives—money, food, promotions, awards, certificates, etc. All of these reinforcers are used to strengthen behaviors considered desirable to the employer or society.

EXHIBIT 5

"The central aspect of a token system is the pairing of teacher praise with tokens which are backed up by an effective reinforcer. In most effective studies, however, many other procedures have also been used. For example, praise for appropriate behavior and ignoring of disruptive behavior are used at times when tokens are not being dispensed. Time out (or isolation) is often used when intensely disruptive behaviors occur. Systematic contingencies in the form of privileges are often applied throughout the day. The children following the rules are the ones who get to help teacher, to be first in line, to choose an activity, etc. The principle of shaping is also systematically applied. Praise, privileges, and tokens are not administered for achieving an absolute standard of performance, but for improving behavior or for maintaining a high level of acceptable behavior (p. 101)."

"A token system is not a magical procedure to be applied in a mechanical way. It is simply one tool within a larger set of tools available to the teacher concerned with improving the behavior of children. The full set of equipment is needed to do the job right (Kuypers, Becker and O'Leary, 1968, p. 108)."

Intrinsic Positive Reinforcement

Intrinsic reinforcers are those available from performing the activity itself. In schools, for example, we assume that the intrinsic reinforcers of satisfaction from knowing, curiosity, novelty, pride in achievement are all operating. It would be difficult, if not impossible, to measure the power of these intrinsic reinforcers for any one child. However, we can assume the intrinsic value of a reinforcer is low if the child does not continue to emit the behavior.

When this is the case, it may be necessary to use an extrinsic reinforcer (social or tangible) to strengthen the desired behavior. The extrinsic reinforcers can be an important first step in strengthening intrinsic reinforcers. Once the behavior is being emitted at a high strength generally the contrived reinforcers can be, and should be, dropped out.

If the assignments in a classroom are set up properly they can easily become reinforcing for *all* children. Performing a task for the intrinsic reinforcement available has been observed in infants as young as three months (e.g., Piaget, 1929) and some lower organisms.

EXHIBIT 6

A series of studies was conducted by Robert Butler and his associates (1953, 1955), to measure task performance with only intrinsic reinforcers available to the animals.

"Each monkey in these studies was placed in a dimly lit, opaque box with two small, covered windows . . . One window was colored yellow and the other blue, with the yellow always locked and the blue unlocked. If the monkey pushed against the blue window it would swing open and permit a view of the laboratory room for 30 seconds. The monkeys not only learned this response for the reward of visual exploration but also showed remarkably little satiation or habituation."

"The strength of this motive depends on the nature of the visual stimulus. The window-opening was less frequent when the reward was an empty room than when a toy train was operating. The strongest reward was the sight of another monkey."

"Sounds were also rewarding. Monkeys responded to hear the train or a monkey, but less frequently than they did to see the train or monkey. Not all stimuli were rewarding. The monkeys did not learn the response in order to see a large dog or hear a monkey in pain (in Murray, 1964, p. 77–78)."

---

6. Positive reinforcement serves the two functions of:
    a. _____ of new behavior.
    b. _____ of behaviors already exhibited.

7. Each time the child misbehaves he is sent to the principal's office. The number of misbehaviors stays at a high rate with this contingency in operation. We might, therefore, assume that going to the principal's office is _____.

8. Learning to write in school so that one can write letters to friends is an example of (extrinsic/intrinsic) reinforcement.

---

6. a. acquisition

    b. maintenance

7. reinforcing (or)
    not aversive

8. intrinsic

9. The following reinforcers can be classified as social, token or intrinsic. Pair each one with the appropriate type of reinforcer.

a. social   b. token and tangible   c. intrinsic

_____(1) praise

_____(2) ice cream

_____(3) feeling of power

_____(4) attention from another person

_____(5) curiosity

_____(6) money

_____(7) gold stars

_____(8) toys

_____(9) success

10. One type of reinforcement, in__*intrinsic*__ reinforcement, is difficult to observe or control. But we can do a great deal with social and token reinforcement to build up desirable behaviors in children.

---

9. (1) a   (4) a   (7) b   10. in*trinsic*

    (2) b   (5) c   (8) b

    (3) c   (6) b   (9) c

SET 3: *Negative Reinforcement*

Negative reinforcement involves the removal of an undesirable or aversive stimulus. This removal of the aversive stimulus serves to strengthen the behavior which removes it.

We generally think of shock, physical pain, and loud noises as aversive. In addition, social interactions such as nagging, scolding, embarrassing and criticizing are generally aversive. For some children with a prior history of pairing aversive events with a person or setting, even the presence of that person or setting can be aversive.

This is what typically happens with an underachieving child. Such a child can develop elaborate and varied techniques for "turning off" such aversive events as oral reading and teacher attention.

Typical techniques which underachieving children use—often with tremendous "success"—include saying "I can't," ignoring teacher initiation, frequent trips to bathroom and drinking fountain, acting out, and in some cases behaviors such as frequent yawning. (Gaasholt, 1969.)

---

11. Presenting a reinforcer following a desirable emitted response is called _____ reinforcement. The termination of an undesirable or aversive event is called _____ reinforcement.

12. A child is teased by a class member. The teasing in this case is aversive to the child; thus we call it a neg_____ reinforcer.

13. Any behavior that terminates the _____ reinforcer will tend to be strengthened and occur again. When the child is teased he hits the teasing classmate. If the teasing stops there is a good chance that hitting behavior has been (weakened, strengthened).

---

11. positive

    negative

12. neg*ative*

13. negative

    strengthened

14. If a sign or comment from the teacher quiets a noisy classroom, then use of the signal is strengthened or maintained because it terminates the negative reinforcer which in this case is the _____.

15. A child wants very badly to be called upon in recitation. So he waves his hand frantically in the air and hops up and down in his chair. To quiet him down the teacher calls on him. This removes the negative reinforcer, _____ _____ for the teacher. Thus one would expect her to (increase, decrease) responding to hand waving.

16. In #15 the teacher is negatively reinforced for calling on the child. What is the effect of her response on the child? His hand waving was _____ and, therefore, will (increase, decrease).

---

14. noisy classroom (or) noise   16. reinforced

15. hand waving   increase

    increase

One of the most important rules in successful behavior change is to reinforce the behavior *immediately* after it occurs. The child in the classroom should be praised (or punished) within seconds after the behavior occurs.

In building or strengthening a behavior, how often reinforcement occurs is also important. Reinforcement which follows each time the behavior or response occurs is called continuous reinforcement.

In general, continuous reinforcement results in learning that behavior more rapidly. Therefore, if a teacher wants to teach a child a certain behavior, she should acknowledge it each time it occurs.

Continuous reinforcement is important in the early stages of behavior acquisition. Once the behavior is well established, however, it is better to reinforce only intermittently.

To systematically reinforce a child it is most effective to set up a schedule of reinforcement. To do this, one decides whether to reinforce the child after a certain period of time (interval schedule) or after a certain number of responses have occurred (ratio schedule). For example, the schedule might specify "reinforce every hour" or it might specify "reinforce every fifth response."

In general an interval schedule maintains consistent behavior over a longer period of time but ratio schedules produce higher rates of responding.

---

17. Sharon is a large, boisterous child who enters the room loudly stomping and yelling each morning. This morning she came in quietly and sat down to read a book. She should be praised within _____ of when she sits down.

18. Ray is a new child in the classroom. Several times the teacher has encouraged him to respond orally with the group but he hides his face and doesn't speak. In a science recitation period

---

17. seconds

he suddenly raises his hand to respond to a question. As the teacher you see your chance to reinforce him by calling on him. He responds—but with the wrong answer. You should:

_____a. praise him after class when the other children have gone.

__✓__b. find something about his response to praise honestly at that moment.

_____c. ignore the comment so it won't draw the other's attention.

19. If a child blurts out comments without raising his hand he can be taught to raise his hand by reinforcing him each time he _____ _____ _____.

20. Continuous reinforcement is important in the early stages when the behavior is being _____. Once the behavior is well established, however, it is better if the reinforcement is intermittent and not _____.

21. When the subject must emit the same behavior several times for reinforcement, the reinforcement schedule is _____. That is, reinforcement does not follow each time the behavior occurs.

22. Once the child raises his hand consistently to respond, he need be praised only periodically for the _____ to maintain.

23. Miss A. teaches 4th grade. A boy in her class has trouble staying in his seat and working. He walks around the room, talks to his

---

18. b	21. intermittent
19. raises his hand	22. behavior (or) response
20. learned, taught (or) acquired	
continuous	

neighbors, looks at the encyclopedias, etc., when the rest of the class is working. Miss A. decides to increase staying-in-seat behavior by praising him and giving attention when he is in his seat working. Since she has a large class to teach she, of course, cannot be with him each time he is working. Therefore, she decides that every 20 minutes she will check his behavior and if he is working she will go praise him. She is reinforcing the boy only after:

    ___✓___a. a certain time interval.

    _____b. the behavior has occurred x number of times.

24. Miss G. has a girl in her 6th grade class who seldom gets her assignments completed to hand in. Therefore, Miss G. decides to make a chart and give her a star each time she hands in a completed assignment, regardless of the amount of time it takes. The schedule of reinforcement Miss G. used is:

    _____a. interval schedule

    ___✓___b. ratio schedule

SUMMARY

1. For maladaptive behavior already present it is more important to look at why the behavior is being maintained—what is happening now—than why it occurred in the first place.

   Remember, in the classroom the behavior may be maintained by the response of the teacher or the other students.

2. Social and token reinforcers are important tools for the teacher in controlling classroom behavior.

3. Removing an aversive stimulus, negative reinforcement, is also important in the classroom.

4. To be effective, reinforcement should follow immediately after the response.

5. When teaching a behavior, it should be rewarded each time it occurs. Once the behavior occurs frequently it should be reinforced only intermittently.

---

23. a   24. b

Section C: How Behaviors Can Be Eliminated

As mentioned in the previous section, there are two basic elements in teaching behavior:

a.   When the behavior is followed immediately by reinforcement the likelihood of that behavior occurring again is *strengthened*.

b.   If a behavior is no longer reinforced that behavior becomes *weaker* in strength.

SET 1: *Punishment*

The use of aversive consequences in eliminating behavior has involved considerable controversy particularly in light of research evidence from some controlled experiments (e.g., Estes, 1944; McClelland, 1951; Lohr, 1959). It should be kept in mind that indeed many behaviors can be eliminated without the use of aversive consequences. Nevertheless, when effectively applied, aversive consequences bring about an abrupt and often complete reduction in response rate. A problem occurs when responses designed to punish deviant behavior do not effectively reduce the frequency and may in some cases accelerate it. Why do teachers and parents continue to use these techniques if they do not decelerate the behavior? Studies have shown that there is often a suppression of the child's behavior at the time of punishment which leads the teacher to believe what he did or said "worked." And when the behavior returns later at a higher intensity we often "blame" it on the child rather than our own behavior.

How often have you heard, "I must tell Brian five times a day to stay in his seat, yet the minute my back is turned helping another child he is out of his seat again"? Such occurrences are good clues the technique is not effective.

What we often speak of as punishment involves physical and/or verbal reprimand for emitting a certain behavior. The significant feature of this "punishment" is that it is *socially* administered rather than a natural contingency of the rules. This physical punishment (spanking, scolding, etc.) generally is administered in an angry, disturbed fashion often accompanied by a verbal barrage from the administrator of the "punishment" (e.g., the teacher).

While "punishment" is often the most frequent type of behavior control used, it has several undesirable side effects:

a. When punished the child may strike back at the object or a socially irrelevant object (e.g., throw a book).

b. The teacher may come to be identified as aversive to the child especially if punishment is meted out in an angry, threatened tone.

c. The effects of punishment have been shown to last for a short time. This is due in part to the inconsistency of "punishment" (depending often on the mood of the teacher).

d. The punished behavior may be suppressed only in the presence of the punishing agent.

The important features to remember in effecting behavior change through punishment are:

a. Specify the rules to the child before the situation occurs, e.g., "The rule at our school is 'no fighting,' anyone found fighting will be sent home for the day."

b. Do not warn or threaten but carry through with the consequence the *first time* and every time the deviant behavior occurs.

c. Make the consequence (e.g., going home) occur immediately following the deviant behavior (e.g., fighting).

d. Make sure the consequence is aversive enough that the child chooses to stop emitting the behavior rather than risk receiving the consequences, e.g., if a child fights so he can be sent home this *would not* be aversive and another technique should be used.

EXHIBIT 7

". . . a low grade on a paper in composition is part of unprogrammed terminal contingencies which do not respect details of the student's behavior and hence do not teach good writing, but a series of small punishments for bad grammar, illogical construction, and solecisms, for example, may be useful (Skinner, 1968, p. 187)."

"If punishment is used, it should be used effectively. . . The humane teacher often resorts to warning the student, 'If you do that again, I will have to punish you.' As a conditioned aversive stimulus, a warning is a mild punishment, but it is also a discriminative stimulus, and a student who is punished only after being warned will discriminate between occasions when behavior is and is not punished and will show the effects of punishment only after a warning has been given (Skinner, 1968, p. 188)."

"What appears to be punishment is sometimes reinforcing; a student misbehaves to annoy his teacher or to be admired by his peers when he takes punishment (Skinner, 1968, p. 190)."

"A fatal principle is 'letting well enough alone'—giving no attention to a student so long as he behaves well and turning to him only when he begins to cause trouble. Under most circumstances, dismissing a class may be reinforcing to the student, but the teacher is likely to dismiss the class when trouble is brewing and thus reinforce early stages of troublemaking (Skinner, 1968, p. 190)."

---

1. A child has been told that his paper is unacceptable and he will have to re-write it before handing it in. As he returns to his desk he kicks the wastebasket which spills. From what you have learned about punishment, is this a likely behavior? (yes, no)

2. At the beginning of school in the fall you get a boy who refuses to work and when you attempt to help him or reason with him

---

1. yes

he gives back "smart talk." Which one of the following *might* account for his behavior:

    _____a. it runs in the family.

    _____b. teachers may have become aversive to him because of his history of punishment.

    _____c. he rejects the school experience; doesn't find it meaningful.

    _____d. he is hyperactive.

3. A rule has been in effect for two weeks that any child who does not complete his work will have to finish it during recess. The rule has been very effective in pushing the production rate of all the students except Jill. She has missed 5 recess periods due to incomplete work. Which of the following may contribute to her non-compliance? (may check more than one)

    _____a. she has a low metabolism.

    _____b. the reinforcer (recess) isn't strong enough.

    _____c. the punishment (lack of recess) isn't strong enough.

    _____d. she likes to cause trouble.

4. One of the goals of education is to develop children with good independent study skills. Mr. James, the principal, is concerned because Miss E.'s classroom behaves well in her presence yet becomes disruptive when she leaves the room. What can be assumed about her control procedures?

    _____a. nothing. All children act up when the teacher is out of the room.

    _____b. her classroom is too permissive.

    _____c. she uses aversive control measures when in the classroom.

    _____d. she is inconsistent in her use of rewards and punishment.

---

2. b

3. b, c

4. c

5. Which one of the following forms of punishment would *not* be effective in eliminating the behavior:

      _____a. a child tries to walk on the teeter-totter, falls and hurts himself.

      _____b. the class is told that one rule is not to walk on teeter-totters, and that anyone found walking on a teeter-totter will lose one recess. The teacher upon finding the boy walking on the teeter-totter simply mentions at the next recess that he will be unable to go out.

      _____c. the child walks on the teeter-totter. Upon seeing this, the teacher shakes him and pulls him along to the side of the building where she stands lecturing him.

---

5. c

SET 2:   *Extinction*

As previously stated, when a behavior is never reinforced it will decrease in strength and may disappear.

The withholding of reinforcement which has previously been contingent upon a behavior is called *extinction*. When the behavior no longer results in the presentation of a reinforcer, the child (or adult) will generally accelerate the frequency and/or magnitude of the behavior in an attempt to produce the reinforcer.

Thus, it is important to remember: with a behavior that we are trying to eliminate by extinction, the response rate may increase after the start of extinction.

How rapidly the behavior is extinguished (decreased) depends on the past reinforcement history of the child. If the child has been intermittently reinforced (see Sec. B.) for a long period of time, it will take a long time to extinguish the behavior. Since most learned behaviors in our environment have been maintained by inconsistent, and thus intermittent, reinforcement it takes patience and consistent non-reinforcement of the behavior to eliminate it from a classroom by extinction.

EXHIBIT 8

Zimmerman and Zimmerman (1966) reported the use of extinction with an 11-year-old boy of normal intelligence. The boy "displayed temper tantrums (kicking, screaming, etc.), spoke baby talk, and incessantly made irrelevant comments or posed irrelevant questions."

Observing a temper tantrum prior to entering the class, "*E* asked the attendant to put the boy in the classroom at his desk and to leave the room. Then *E* closed the door. The boy sat at his desk, kicking and screaming; *E* proceeded to her desk and worked there, ignoring *S*-2. After 2 or 3 min. the boy, crying softly, looked up at *E*. Then *E* announced that she would be ready to work with him as soon as he indicated that he was ready to work. He continued to cry and scream with diminishing loudness for the next 4 or 5 min. Finally, he lifted his head and stated that he was ready. Immediately, *E* looked up at him, smiled, went to his desk, and said, 'Good, now let's get to work.' The boy worked quietly and cooperatively with *E* for the remainder of the class period."

"After several weeks [repeating this procedure with each tantrum], class tantrums disappeared entirely (p. 95)."

6. If a child is aware he is making a noise in the classroom by loudly tapping his pencil and the noise goes unnoticed—peers as well as teacher ignore the behavior—it will probably _____.

7. In the example of the pencil tapping child, if the teacher uses the process of extinction she no longer acknowledges his behavior as disruptive and she has told the other children not to turn around and pay attention. Thus the child's reward for pencil tapping has been cut off and he may tap even louder to get the attention. It is important that the teacher not acknowledge the tapping regardless of the loudness because any acknowledgment will _____ the new intensity.

8. The process of ex_____ also works on desirable behaviors. A child comes in each morning and sits in his chair quietly ready for work while the rest of the group is loud and talking. If no one notices and comments—either teacher or peers—then he will probably stop coming in quietly and start talking like the rest of the class. In this case his quiet appropriate behavior has been _____.

9. Extinction can be used effectively with which one of the following behaviors:
   _____a. attempted strangling of peers.
   ___✓__b. asking irrelevant questions.
   _____c. femininity in male student.
   _____d. swearing and coarse language.

---

6. decrease, stop, terminate (or) drop out.

8. ex*tinction*

   extinguished

7. reinforce (or) reward

9. b

10. Which reasons explain why extinction would not be effective with the other three behaviors in #9:

     _____a. difficult to remove reinforcers.

     _____b. not operant behavior.

     _____c. possible acceleration of behavior unwise.

     _____d. a and c above.

---

10. d

SET 3: *Time-out (TO)*

For some behaviors, simply ignoring the child is not enough to curtail the behavior without excessive expenditure of time. For these behaviors, time-out from positive reinforcement represents an effective alternative (e.g., Walker, Mattson, & Buckley, 1969; Bijou, Birnbrauer, Kidder & Tague, 1967).

The method of time-out removes the child from a situation in which he can receive reinforcement. This differs from extinction in that the method of extinction removes the reinforcing stimulus rather than the child.

Generally this method utilizes a time-out room (sometimes called a "quiet room"). The child is requested to go to the time-out room for a period of time (usually 10 minutes). The room is devoid of interesting objects so that during this period he talks to no one, has nothing to play with, and no academic assignment. If ready to begin work after that time he may return to the room. It is important that the teacher not lecture or scold the child or let her expression show she is upset. Often getting a teacher upset is reinforcing to a child and is "worth" suffering aversive consequences.

EXHIBIT 9

In a study by Tyler and Brown (1967) time-out procedures were used with fifteen delinquent boys, ages 13–15. The setting involved a training school cottage for boys committed by the courts.

The behaviors the experimenters attempted to alter were misbehaviors at the pool table—including "breaking the rules of the game, throwing pool cues, scuffling, kibitzing and bouncing balls on the floor."

The three phases of the study included:

Phase I: (7 weeks), "misbehavior resulted in *S* being immediately confined in a 'time-out' room for 15 min."

Phase II: (13 weeks), "*S* was verbally reprimanded."

Phase III: (20 weeks), time-out reinstated.

During Phases I & III, "every time an *S* misbehaved in any . . . [way], he was immediately placed in the time-out room for 15 min. There were to be no warnings, no discussions, no arguments and no second chances. When an *S* misbehaved, he was simply taken in a very matter-of-fact way to the time-out room."

Following Phase I, "a No Punishment condition . . . was instituted to observe the effects on behavior . . . When an *S* misbehaved, the staff member would mildly reprimand him with a statement such as 'Now cut it out,' 'I'm warning you,' 'Don't let that happen again,' etc."

"The clear trend in the data was that as *S*s were punished for their misbehavior, this behavior declined in rate; when punishment was not administered, the behavior increased in rate. All fifteen *S*s showed this pattern (p. 1–3)."

---

11. If used properly, making a child sit in a corner for misbehavior is an example of (extinction, time-out).

12. To be effective there must be no desirable stimuli for the child when placed in time-out. Check any of the following statements which would be a way to use time-out.
    ___✓__a. placing a child in a room with only a chair and blank walls.
    _____b. placing a child in the hallway.
    _____c. placing the child in the front corner of the classroom, as an example to the rest of the class.
    _____d. sending a child to the principal's office to do odd jobs.

13. The effectiveness of time-out depends on an alternate response being available for reinforcement. If the environment is not reinforcing to the child, putting him in isolation is not aversive.

---

11. time-out

12. a (all others may give chance for reinforcement)

Which of the following children might respond well to the time-out techniques? (may check more than one answer).

   ✓ a. a child who enjoys math, placed in time-out during math.

   ✓ b. a child who talks and giggles with his peers.

       c. a withdrawn child.

       d. a child who enjoys math, placed in time-out during reading.

---

13. a & b

SET 4: *Reinforcing Incompatible Behaviors (Counterconditioning)*

Incompatible behaviors are behaviors which are difficult to perform simultaneously with the deviant behavior. When these behaviors are being performed they do not allow for maladaptive behaviors to occur. This procedure is illustrated by the frequent technique of giving a lost, crying child an ice cream cone. The child cannot be crying and enjoying the ice cream cone at the same time.

Reinforcing incompatible behaviors is a useful tool for eliminating undesirable behaviors and building up desirable behaviors. It increases the effectiveness of other reinforcement or punishment techniques when used in conjunction with them. Thus it will be doubly effective if we reinforce in-seat behavior at the same time that we punish out-of-seat behavior.

In some cases where it is difficult to work with the deviant behavior, working with an incompatible behavior may be more profitable. The problem of truancy illustrates this. If we only punish the child for not coming to school we may increase his dislike for school. Yet if reinforcers were used, it would seem unfair to reinforce him for just coming to school. A better alternative would be to make coming to school desirable. The teacher can determine what would make school desirable—less frustrating assignments (or conversely, more challenging assignments), changes in text, earned privileges, teacher attention, etc.—and make this available to the child.

EXHIBIT 10

The authors used the technique of reinforcing incompatible behaviors in a study of conditioning attending behavior (Walker & Buckley, 1968).

"Phillip was a bright (WISC: 116), underachieving male who, upon referral, exhibited a number of deviant behaviors that were incompatible with successful, task-oriented performance in the classroom setting. Phillip was enrolled in the fourth grade and his chronological age at referral was 9–6. His deviant behaviors in the classroom reportedly included verbally and physically provoking other children, not completing tasks, making loud noises and comments, coercing attention from the teacher, talking out of turn, and being easily distracted from a given task by ordinary classroom stimuli such as minor noises, movements of others, changes in lighting conditions, and a number of other stimuli common to a classroom setting. A series of observations from the regular classroom... indicated he attended to assignments only 42% of the time."

During treatment phase the "subject was told that when a given interval of time had elapsed, in which no distractions had occurred, a click would sound and the experimenter would enter a single check mark in a cumulative recording form which would indicate that the subject had earned a point. The subject was told that attending to the click represented a distraction and would result in loss of the point for that interval. The subject was allowed to exchange his points for a model of his choice at the conclusion of the treatment period."

"Systematic manipulation of the reinforcement contingency during the individual conditioning program produced significant changes in the response measures of percentage of attending behavior and frequency and duration of non-attending behavioral events. Upon withdrawal of the reinforcement contingency, the behavior returned to pretreatment levels, thus indicating that the alteration in behavior was due to the manipulated, experimental variable rather than to the influence of an unknown or chance variable."

Once the behaviors were under experimental control, procedures were established for programming generalization and maintenance of the behavior outside the experimental setting (p. 245—250).

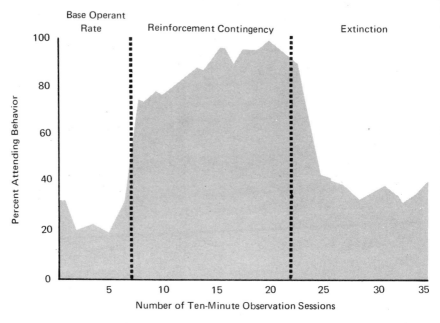

Fig. 2. Percentage of attending behavior in successive time samples during the individual conditioning program.

---

14. Examples of incompatible behaviors in class are:
    a. distractive behavior and (talking, working on task)
    b. whispering to peer and (responding to teacher, out-of-seat)
    c. reading a comic book and (singing, leaning back in chair)

15. For a child who has a high rate of non-attending, distractive behavior, reinforcement for _____ should reduce the number of distractions.

---

14. a. working on task
    b. responding to
       teacher
    c. singing

15. working on task (or)
    attending to task

16. Mr. T. is using time-out for each time Bill talks back rudely. At the same time he can give smiles and praise when Bill _____.

17. Mrs. S. has several students that shout out answers during discussion. She is trying to eliminate "talk·outs" by ignoring those children and only responding to children with raised hands. She will get even more rapid results if when a child remembers to raise his hand she _____ him.

---

16. responds properly (or) isn't rude

17. praises (or) reinforces

Satiation is the method of presenting a reinforcing stimulus at such a high rate that it is no longer desirable and may be aversive. Having a child write 500 times a dirty word which he has used is an example of the technique of satiation. What was desirable to say once becomes undesirable after repeating it 500 times.

Due to the differences in satiation level both among subjects and among reinforcers, it is difficult to determine the effectiveness of this technique. In some cases it effectively curtails the behavior and in others the effects are only short term. When physiological reinforcers, novel reinforcers, or conditioned reinforcers are involved it is difficult to use satiation.

The process of satiation, however, should be kept in mind particularly since desirable behaviors are sometimes inadvertently diminished through satiation of a reinforcer (Landau & Gewirtz, 1967).

EXHIBIT 11

Teodoro Ayllon (1963) used the procedure of stimulus satiation with a female mental patient. The patient had a nine-year history of towel collecting and storing when they were made available to her. It was reported that about twice a week the nurses simply removed the towels from the patient's room.

With the beginning of the experiment the nurses stopped removing the towels. Instead they gave towels to the patient without comment intermittently throughout the day. The number of towels given her per day was increased from seven the first week to an average of 60 per day by the third week.

The author reports, "During the first few weeks of satiation, the patient was observed patting her cheeks with a few towels, apparently enjoying them." By the fourth and fifth weeks the patient exhibited comments such as "Get these dirty towels out of here." After the total towels in the room reached 625, the patient began voluntarily removing them. This continued until she had almost no towels and maintained for the next 12 months at 1.5 towels per week.

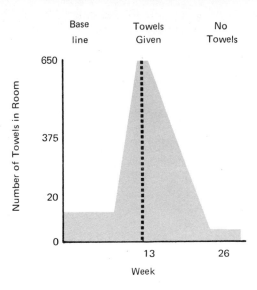

Fig. 3. "A response, towel hoarding, is eliminated when the patient is given towels in excess . . ." (Ayllon, 1963)

---

18. A child who tips back in his chair frequently is annoying to most teachers. One method of eliminating the behavior is by satiation. If the child is forced to lean back in his chair all day and to come down under no circumstances except leaving the room, we can expect the behavior of leaning back to (increase, decrease) according to the theory of _____.

19. If a child is required to practice on the piano for great lengths of time each day, what once was fun (reinforcing) may become _____ through satiation.

---

18. decrease   19. aversive

    satiation

20. If satiation of a reinforcer is taking place the child's behavior which obtains the reinforcer will (increase, decrease).

21. If a grade school child is required to perform the behaviors listed below for an extended period of time, which three of the behaviors could we expect to no longer be reinforcing to the child:

_____a. T. V. watching
_____b. pencil sharpening
_____c. standing to work
_____d. eating food
_____e. crawling on floor
_____f. stealing money

---

20. decrease   21. b, c, e

SET 6: *(Simple) Stimulus Change*

Certain responses seem to occur only when specific conditions are present. Thus, by altering the conditions we can eliminate the behavior.

Stimulus change is simply the process of changing the environmental contingencies, i.e., stimulus(i), to reduce the chances of the behavior occurring.

The technique of stimulus change is very common in the regular classroom. If a child continually pokes at the student next to him the teacher generally moves his desk away. By moving the desk the teacher is changing the stimulus that brought about the poking.

Stimulus change has the short term effect of terminating undesirable behavior. Yet if the stimulus conditions are returned to the original state (e.g., the child's desk is moved back) there is a chance the maladaptive behavior will *reappear*.

---

22. When a child giggles and talks in the back of the line while going to gym class or the lunch room by placing him at the front of the line the teacher usually stops the giggling and talking. This is an example of _____ change. The stimulus in this case is (proximity to friends and distance from teacher, giggling and talking).

23. For a child who sucks his thumb, gloves can be placed on his hands to prevent the *response* of _____ _____.

---

22. stimulus

    proximity to friends and
    distance from teacher

23. thumb sucking

51

24. Adaptive school behaviors can be affected by stimulus change as well as maladaptive behaviors. A well known example is the child who knows his lines for the school play very well but forgets them in front of the audience. The change in stimuli, in this case _____, produced a change in the child's behavior (response).

25. Name the six techniques mentioned for decreasing deviant behavior.

1._____   4._____
2._____   5._____
3._____   6._____ change

SUMMARY

In this section a variety of techniques for decreasing or eliminating deviant behavior were discussed. They include:

1. "Punishment"—physical and/or verbal reprimand by a social agent.
2. Extinction—withholding the reinforcement for the behavior.
3. Reinforcing behaviors incompatible with maladaptive behavior.
4. Time-out—removing the child from the reinforcing climate.
5. Satiation—presenting a desirable stimulus at such a high rate that it loses its reinforcing value and may become aversive.
6. Stimulus change—altering the environment so that the eliciting stimulus is no longer present.

The type of technique a teacher chooses for any one behavior will depend on the seriousness of the misbehavior, how often it occurs, and practical matters such as length of time needed, adaptability to classroom, and reaction of parents, peers and students.

---

24. audience size   25. (see Summary)

Section D: Measuring Behavior

SET 1: *What Behaviors to Measure*

Before we can ask WHY a child is behaving as he is, we need to ask WHAT he is doing and HOW OFTEN the behavior occurs.

In observing a child it is important not to imply motives or feelings from the behaviors. It is only guessing to say a child "looks guilty," "hates his teacher," "is lazy," "is hyperactive," etc. The maladaptive behaviors a child exhibits should be described in terms of events that can be easily counted and recorded.

Not only should implying behaviors be avoided but also trying to find causes. After looking at the behavior, we can assume why it occurs but we must be willing to change that assumption when we get feedback from our recordings or raw data.

Once the behavior has been described as something that can be observed and recorded it is necessary to specify the dimensions of the behavioral category. The category should be defined so that any time the child emits a behavior you can easily say the behavior does or does not fall within the category. Some classroom behaviors such as talking out, not completing assignments, and tardiness can be easily defined. Behaviors such as sloppy writing, smart talk, silly behavior, non-attending, are more difficult to define.

The criterion for the category may vary with the behavior, the setting and the child. What may be defined as noisy in the classroom would be considered "normal" on the playground.

In a study by the authors (Walker & Buckley, 1968) the following observable behaviors were classified as non-attending events: "(a) looking away from the text and answer sheet by eye movements or head turning; (b) bringing an object into his field of vision with head and eyes directed toward paper (other than pencil, book and answer sheet necessary for the task); and (c) making marks other than those necessary for the task (e.g., doodling) (p. 246)."

1. Before recording behaviors, the behaviors must be stated in concrete or _____ terms and the limits of the category specified.

2. "The child enters the room following the final bell to begin class" describes (lazy habits, tardiness).

3. Which of the following are concrete observations:
   ____a. he is frustrated by math.
   ____b. he throws incomplete math papers in the waste-basket.
   ____c. he has an inferiority complex.
   ____d. he comments that no one likes him.
   ____e. he frequently does not participate in PE.
   ____f. he is lazy.

4. Dan disrupts the classroom frequently by banging his desk. His teacher decides to count the number of occurrences. His behavior could best be counted by recording:
   ____a. attention getting events.
   ____b. hostility.
   ____c. banging on desk.
   ____d. insecure behavior.

---

1. observable

2. tardiness

3. b, d, e

4. c

5. "Noise: Whenever the student is talking loudly, yelling or making other deliberate inappropriate noises—such as banging books or scraping chair back and forth—which is actually or potentially disruptive to others."* This description of noisy behavior (could, could not) be used effectively to record such behaviors.

---

*Code category from observation form developed by R. S. Ray, D. A. Shaw and G. R. Patterson, Oregon Research Institute, 1968.

---

5. could

Not only is it important to describe behaviors in observable terms, it is also important to tell how often the behavior occurs.

The statement "he throws incomplete math papers into the wastebasket" becomes more precise by "he threw four incomplete out of ten assigned math papers into the wastebasket in the last two weeks."

Scientists have found that our own estimations of how often a behavior occurs are extremely inaccurate when compared with actual recordings. For example, an extremely annoying behavior may seem to occur more frequently than it actually does.

It is useful in dealing with some behaviors to take recordings on a classroom peer as well. What may seem like a high rate of "silly" behavior by a first grader may be a rather typical response exhibited by his peers as well. If he is not producing the behavior at a higher rate, yet it is still *more* annoying, we need to look at other variables involved.

The level at which a response normally occurs before we intervene is called the operant level. The period of recording this operant level is called the baseline period.

Because our own estimations are inaccurate, taking baseline recordings before we start to change behaviors is essential to determining the success of our technique.

After several days of taking baseline recordings, the teacher is ready to begin her treatment procedure. Recordings should be continued during this time. If the intervention technique is later stopped, the recording should continue at infrequent intervals as a check on maintenance of good performance in the child (follow-up recordings).

---

6. Recordings taken before starting to change a child's behavior are called _____ recordings.

7. Baseline recordings are essential to knowing the _____ of intervention.

---

6. baseline 7. results/success

8. Recordings can be divided into three phases in relation to treating or intervening in a problem. These three phases are:

    a.

    b.

    c.

---

8.   a. baseline (pre-, before)
    b. treatment phase (intervention phase, during)
    c. follow-up (post phase, after)

SET 3: *How to Record Behaviors*

Behavior recording, when efficient, requires very little time. There are a variety of efficient methods for recording behaviors. The common element in all of them is consistency. The small amount of time expended in getting accurate and consistent recordings will be paid for by improvement in the child's behavior.

Probably the easiest way to record behaviors is to simply tally the behavior each time it occurs. The only prerequisite for keeping such tallies is that the behavior be clearly defined in observable terms so that you know what to include.

Continuous recording of each behavioral event (*frequency count*) is best used for behaviors that are discrete units occurring less than 20 times a day. (Discrete is used to describe units of behavior that are easily defined as separate and distinct.)

Other recording techniques must be used for behaviors that occur at extremely high rates, are difficult to continuously observe, or cannot be broken down into small discrete units.

A technique called *time sampling* can be used to record behaviors that occur at high rates, or are difficult to observe over time. Time-sampling involves recording behavior at certain times during the day rather than continuously. This method will give an accurate count of behaviors when extended over long periods of time.

In using the time sampling technique predetermined times should be set up to observe the behavior. The length of each recording period depends on the specific behavior. Accurate recordings could be made by recording the first five minutes of each hour, fifteen minute blocks three times a day, or ½ hour each day.

When the time period over which the behavior occurs varies from day to day a useful technique for recording is to compute the *rate* at which the behavior occurs. Rate is computed by dividing the number of behaviors by the length of time the behavior is recorded.

For behaviors which occur for long periods of time and which are hard to break into discrete units, the *duration* of the behavior can be recorded. The duration is the period of time during which each separate instance of the behavior occurs.

Thus length of each behavior might be recorded for behaviors such as "in-seat behavior," independent reading, or transition between subject areas.

9. Recording behavior only at specified time intervals during the day is called time sampling technique as opposed to _____ recording of each response.

10. Observing the child only once a day for 15 minutes is also an example of the time _____ technique.

11. Time sampling is useful with behaviors difficult for a classroom teacher to record continuously all day such as:
    _____a. non-attending.
    _____b. muscle tics.
    _____c. eye-blinking.
    _____d. nail-biting.
    _____e. babbling.
    _____f. all of the above.

12. If a teacher looks at the child every hour—9:00, 10:00, etc.—and notes whether the behavior is present or absent she (is, is not) using the time sampling technique.

13. A teacher observes a child for ten minutes and the behavior she wants to change, accelerate or decelerate, occurs four times during that period. To obtain the rate per minute she divides 4 by 10. The behavior occurred _____ times per minute.

14. A child completes 17 arithmetic problems in eight minutes. His production rate is _____ problems per minute.

---

9. continuous

10. sampling

11. f

12. is

13. .40

14. 2.1

15. If a child gets out of his chair frequently and moves around the room we can record number of times out-of-seat (frequency recording) or amount of time in-seat which is a way of recording _____.

---

15. duration

SET 4: *Interpreting Recordings*

The recording aspect of behavioral alteration cannot be over-emphasized. There are many techniques available which effect changes in behavior. Therefore, it is possible, even with the use of a "good" technique, to not effect the desired change or even accelerate maladaptive behavior. Without data the treatment program cannot be critically evaluated and altered.

Transferring the raw data to graphs facilitates reading the data. Two easily used graphs are the bar graph (frequency histogram) and the line graph (frequency polygon). A line graph is generally used because of the ease of making and reading one. The vertical and horizontal axes should be clearly labeled as to the behavior recorded. It is a matter of practice that the vertical axis represents the behavior being counted and the horizontal axis the number of observation periods.

The placement of observations from all three phases (baseline, treatment and follow-up) on the same graph facilitates comparison. These three phases can be separated by vertical dotted lines on the frequency polygon.

---

16. During one week a behavior is observed to occur 5, 8, 12, 15, 14 times. Plot the points on the bar graph below.

15 |
10 |
5 |
0 |
    1   2   3   4   5

Observations

16.

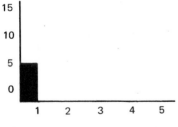

17. A classroom teacher has recorded number of times out of seat each day for one child. Label the axes for her recordings:

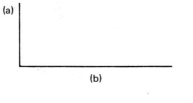

(a)

(b)

a._____   b._____

18. The child was out of his seat 10 times the first day, 13 the second and 8 the third. Plot the data points on the frequency polygon below:

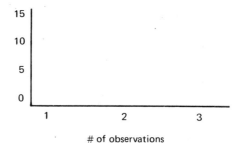

Times out-of-seat

# of observations

---

17. a. number of times
       out of seat

    b. number of
       observations (days)

18.

19. Mr. N. is recording number of arithmetic problems correct for each child. He is also interested in the amount of time required to finish the problems each day. Therefore, he is going to use rate (in this case number of correct problems per minute). His data for Phillip show:

No. Correct	Time to Complete
15	2 min.
7	1 min.
18	4 min.

Plot the three data points on the graph below:

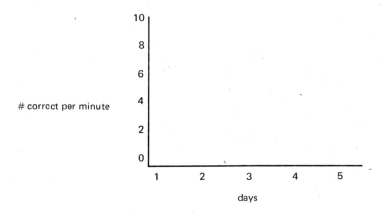

\# correct per minute

days

19.

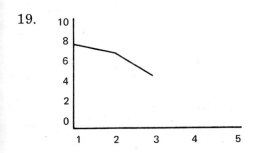

20. In the graph below the teacher has divided the data with a dotted vertical line each time she began a new phase. Assuming the data is complete, label the three phases.

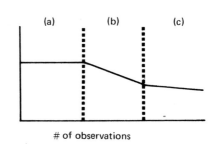

a. _____

b. _____

c. _____

21. Based on the graph in #20 did the teacher's treatment procedure work? (yes, no)

_____

20. a. baseline   21. yes
    b. treatment
    c. follow-up

22. Assume that you are trying to increase the number of problems correct out of 10 for a child. The graph from your recording looks as follows:

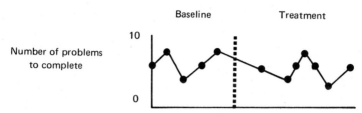

From the basis of the data should you continue the procedure? (yes, no) Explain.

23. Miss V. has a child who sings or hums to himself and disturbs the children around him. She decided to use *extinction* and told the children to ignore him when he is singing or humming. Her data thus far appear below. Should she continue the procedure? (yes, no)

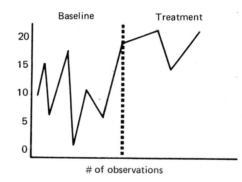

22. No—No change occurring. One should not continue unless there is some reason to believe the program had not been in effect long enough to get change.

23. yes (see p. 38)

24. The following is a graph of fighting behavior for a fourth grade boy.

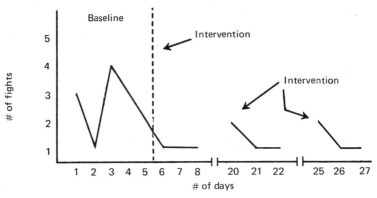

"omission of days (e.g. 9-19 omitted, 23-24 omitted)

From the data, what technique has been used?
_____a. extinction
_____b. punishment
_____c. token reinforcement

SUMMARY

1. It is important to record behavior in observable terms without implying motives or causes.
2. Methods of recording adaptable to classroom use are:
   a. frequency
   b. time-sampling
   c. rate
   d. duration
3. The behavior of the child should be recorded prior to intervention, during intervention and following intervention (if the intervention technique is terminated).

---

24. b. cues: (abrupt change with intervention.

   Reappearance of behavior over time)

EXHIBIT 12

The following study (Bijou, 1966) illustrates many of the procedures discussed in Part I.

"The subject, Ann, was above average intelligence and came from a family in the upper-middle socioeconomic class. After 6 weeks in the nursery school, which is considered the normal period required for adaptation, it was noted that she spent a small part of her time with children. Most of her time was spent with adults or alone, sometimes in constructive occupation, other times just sitting and standing about. Most of her time with adults was devoted to trying to attract the teacher's attention with her collection of rocks, pieces of wood, etc., and talking about her scratches, bumps, and bruises. Her speech was hesitant and low, and at times she showed tic-like behaviors.

"Two trained observers recorded Ann's behaviors each morning under the regular and usual conditions of school attendance. With the exception of snack time, time spent with children and time spent with adults was recorded at 10-second intervals over 5 mornings. Data derived provided a baseline and information on the reliability of the raters. Over the 5-day period Ann spent about 10 percent of her time with children and about 40 percent with adults.

"On day 6, one of the teachers was assigned to go to Ann immediately and remain with her and her group as long as she was with children. Under these circumstances the teacher watched, commented favorably on Ann's play and especially the play activity of the group. The teacher was also instructed to give Ann minimal or no attention when she was alone or with adults, including the teacher herself. Under these conditions, which were in effect for 6 days (day 6 to day 11), Ann spent about 60 percent of the mornings in play with her peers and less than 20 percent in contact with adults.

"On day 12, and the 5 succeeding days, the contingencies were reversed, that is, the baseline conditions were again reinstated. During this period (day 12 to day 16) interactions with children fell to about 20 percent and interactions with adults rose to about 40 percent.

"On day 17, and during the succeeding 8 days, the teacher again reinforced Ann for contact and play with peers. Over this time span, play with children stabilized at about 60 percent, and contacts with adults at about 25 percent. Adult attention for interaction with children was gradually made more intermittent, and the schedule of nonreinforcement of adult contacts was gradually relaxed during the last days of this period.

"Six days (day 31) after the last day of the study (day 25) the first post-study check was made to see whether the changes persisted. Other checks were made on the thirteenth, fifteenth, and twenty-sixth days after completion of the main study. These data showed that the changes were maintained in that Ann was spending about 54 percent of her mornings with children and about 18 percent with adults (pp. 63–64)."

Part II: Application

Section E: Modifying Classroom Behavior

SET 1: *Behavior Change*

Behavioral events can be classified as either of a covert or overt nature. Covert behavior is made up of phenomena such as feelings, attitudes, and emotional states which are not subject to direct observation and validation. Since it cannot be observed directly, covert behavior is very difficult to measure in a scientifically precise or reliable fashion. In discussing the measurement of human behavior, for example, Skinner (1953) notes that the reliable validation of such internal feeling states represents an improbable if not an impossible task.

The existence of overt behavioral events, on the other hand, can be documented through the processes of direct observation and measurement. Hilgard (1962) has defined overt behavior as, "Those activities of an organism that can be observed by another organism or by an experimenter's instruments." (p. 614) This definition suggests that it is possible for overt behaviors to be observed and recorded by independent observers with some degree of reliability. Overt responses in the laboratory such as lever pressing and disc pecking in animal research are usually recorded automatically on instruments designed for this purpose. Most human behavior would be classified as overt since it is observable and therefore subject to quantification and measurement through direct recording procedures.*

Behavior change is defined as an *observable* alteration in overt behavior. A change in behavior may be due to some internal physiological state or it may be a result of an abrupt environmental change. In this instance, we can say that an observable alteration in behavior has occurred even though we may not be able to specify the cause of the behavior change.

---

*Direct recording procedures as discussed in Section D.

In recording changes in overt behavior, it is important to describe the exact nature of the change(s) which has occurred. For example, does the change occur in the behavioral event's rate, in its form, in its variability, in its duration, or in some combination of these factors. In precise measurement, the type of behavior change is equally as important as the fact of behavior change. Behavior technology thus attempts to program changes in overt behavior and to precisely describe the nature of these changes.

---

1. Research studies by Eysenck, (1952, 1960) and Levitt (1957, 1963) have shown that traditional methods of psychotherapy are no more effective than the passage of _____ in producing behavior _____.

2. Behavior change is defined as an *observable* alteration in overt behavior. A shift in a child's emotional state (would, would not) be defined as behavior change.

3. Behavior change is not represented in the example (in #2) above because there was a shift in the child's _____ state which (is, is not) an observable change in _____ behavior.

4. Research studies have demonstrated that while internal feeling states exercise control over some human activities, they are not _____ predictors of changes in overt behavior.

---

1. time
   change

2. would not

3. emotional
   is not
   overt

4. effective, reliable, good (or) valid

5. Conversely, research has shown that environmental events such as reinforcing and aversive stimuli exercise powerful _____ over overt behavior.

6. Traditional psychotherapy manipulates internal feeling states, attitudes, emotions, feelings, in order to produce _____ in overt behavior.

7. Behavior technology manipulates (external, internal) environmental events so as to produce changes in overt behavior.

8. Traditional psychotherapy is based upon the medical or disease model. The cause of the behavior pathology would thus reside (within, outside) the affected individual.

9. Behavior technology is based upon a learning theory model since it assumes that the deviant behavior is _____ as a result of the environmental events that are applied to that behavior.

---

5. control

6. changes

7. external

8. within

9. learned (or) acquired

SET 2: *Therapeutic Application of Operant Theory*

The strength of behavioral events can be measured by noting how frequently they occur over time. If bar pressing rate is 2.00 (occurs twice a minute) and disc pecking rate is .50 (occurs once every two minutes) then bar pressing is at higher strength than disc pecking since it occurs more frequently. Children in the classroom produce behavior(s) which are at high strength and which are also highly variable in both form and rate. These behaviors can be classified along such dimensions as overt/covert, high rate/low rate, and appropriate/inappropriate for purposes of analysis and description.

The teacher is usually most concerned with those child behaviors that are at high rates, which are of an overt nature, and are inappropriate to successful classroom performance. She often spends large amounts of her time and energy in attempts at controlling these behaviors. This management problem is further complicated by the fact that these behaviors are of such high strength that the teacher's control over them is usually only temporary. Examples of such behavior would include general hyperactivity, talking out, short attention span, disturbing others, daydreaming, temper tantrum, wandering around the room, etc. The teacher's goal is not to completely eradicate these behaviors from the child's repertoire but to reduce their rates to manageable proportions within the classroom setting.

The behaviors described above are non-productive in the classroom setting since they disrupt the instructional process and actively compete with successful academic performance. The goal of effective classroom management would be to weaken or suppress these competing behaviors in order to facilitate the learning process. In behavior technology, there are a number of techniques which can be used to reduce the frequency of inappropriate classroom behavior. When these techniques are applied to maladaptive (deviant) behavior in an effort to weaken that behavior, we refer to a therapeutic application of learning theory principles. Methods of weakening a behavior include extinction, cost contingency, time-out, physical restraint, and counter-conditioning.

10. The primary goal of therapeutic applications is to _____ maladaptive behavior. Listed below are four commonly used methods of weakening behavior. Which of the following would not weaken a maladaptive behavior?
      _____a. to reinforce a competing response which is incompatible with the deviant behavior.
      _____b. physical suppression which prevents the response from occurring.
      _____c. attempting to control the disruptive effects of the deviant behavior by "talking the child out of it."
      _____d. withholding reinforcement from the deviant behavior.

11. Physical restraint, which is designed to suppress the behavior to which it is applied, would be *in*appropriate with which of the following: (May check more than one)
      _____a. extreme hyperactivity.
      _____b. out-of-seat behavior.
      _____c. non-attending.
      _____d. overt aggression.
      _____e. talking-out.

12. The use of physical restraint in controlling maladaptive behavior must, necessarily, be of (long, short) term duration.

13. Instead of using physical restraint after the behavior has occurred, a better procedure would be to program the environment so as to _____ a reoccurrence of the inappropriate behavior.

---

10. weaken, reduce (or) remove   12. short
    c

11. b, c, e   13. prevent (or) preclude

14. A number of classroom behaviors such as tapping pencils, not working, daydreaming, disturbing others, talking out, etc., are classified as teacher irritants. These behaviors are often maintained by the _____ which they elicit from the teacher.

15. If a teacher scolds, frowns at, or warns a child each time he talks out, she may be (weakening, strengthening) the very behavior she is trying to (weaken, strengthen).

16. If the teacher suspects that her attention is maintaining talk outs, she could test this assumption by systematically _____ her attention from the behavior.

17. If talking out showed a sudden increase following withdrawal of attention and then a gradual decline in rate, the teacher would have established a (functional, non-functional) relationship between her attention and talking out.

18. The process by which behavior is weakened through withdrawal of reinforcement is known as _____.

19. When an aversive stimulus follows deviant behavior, that behavior is said to have been _____.

---

14. attention, response (or) reinforcer

15. strengthening weaken

16. withholding (or) varying

17. functional

18. extinction

19. punished

20. The function of an aversive stimulus is to (strengthen, weaken) the behavior which it follows.

21. The occurrence of the deviant response is then usually _____ in the presence of the aversive stimulus.

22. In punishment, an aversive stimulus is added to the situation. In extinction a _____ stimulus is withheld from the organism in the conditioning situation—it is subtracted from the situation.

23. In punishment, an aversive stimulus follows the deviant response and is added to the situation. In extinction, a (positive, negative) reinforcer is withheld or subtracted from the conditioning situation.

24. In some conditioning programs, the individual can earn positive reinforcers for producing appropriate behavior and can *lose* a portion of his earned reinforcers for producing _____ behavior.

25. Response cost or cost contingency is a form of punishment where earned _____ are subtracted upon the production of deviant behavior.

---

20. weaken

21. suppressed, inhibited (or) withheld

22. reinforcing (or) positive

23. positive

24. inappropriate

25. reinforcers (or) tokens

26. Laboratory studies have demonstrated that this technique is very _____ in weakening behavior.

27. Suppose that a child is being reinforced, on an interval basis, for inhibiting socially aggressive behavior. He receives an average of ten points per day for *not* producing this form of deviant behavior. His favorite activity is building model airplanes. You tell him that when he accumulates a hundred points, he can exchange them for a model of his choice. By the fourth day, he has earned thirty-five points toward the model. However, you observe him attacking a smaller child on the playground. You could respond to this situation in several ways:
    a. you could withhold reinforcement for a period of time.
    b. you could tell the child he can't earn points if he doesn't learn to suppress his aggressive behavior.
    c. you could ignore the incident.
    d. you could subtract ten of his thirty-five points as a result of the incident.

28. Which of the options in #27 uses response cost? _____

29. Which response in #27 would probably terminate the aggressive behavior in the shortest period of time? _____

30. In d (#27), the teacher is applying a(n) _____ stimulus to the aggressive behavior. This would be a form of _____.

---

26. effective (or) efficient

27. (no response necessary)

28. d

29. d

30. aversive (or) unpleasant

    punishment

31. Time-out is another form of _punishment_ where the child is removed from a reinforcing situation contingent upon the production of deviant behavior.

32. If the situation from which the child is removed is not _interesting_ for him, time-out (will, will not) be effective in weakening the deviant behavior which it follows.

33. If a child would rather be in the classroom among his classmates than removed from the room, time-out could be used contingently to _____ a variety of inappropriate behaviors.

34. During time-out, a period of from ten to fifteen minutes is usually sufficient. However, some children may require a longer period of time before it becomes _successful_.

35. There are a number of appropriate responses which are counter to or (compatible, incompatible) with inappropriate responses. Examples would include fighting versus not fighting, attending versus non-attending, sitting still versus movement around the room, etc.

36. When we reinforce a response which is incompatible with the response we are attempting to weaken, we are using a technique known as counter-_conditioning_.

---

31. punishment

32. reinforcing, rewarding (or) pleasant

    will not

33. weaken, suppress (or) eradicate

34. effective (or) efficient

35. incompatible

36. conditioning

37. Counter-conditioning is effective in weakening deviant behavior and in _____ appropriate behavior.

38. In attempting to control the behavior of an extremely hyperactive child, we could _____-condition responses which compete with hyperactivity such as attending to task, not talking out, working quietly, remaining in seat, etc.

39. We could also use a combination of reinforcing and aversive techniques by rewarding/strengthening the competing responses and _____/weakening the hyperactivity.

40. Using a combination of positive and aversive techniques would probably effect the desired behavior change within a (shorter, longer) period of time.

---

37. strengthening

38. counter

39. punishing

40. shorter

SET 3: *Prosthetic Application*

While the acting out, disruptive child poses a serious management problem for the teacher, children who are extremely withdrawn, or those who have severe academic deficits present an even more rigorous challenge to the teacher's skill. These children are not behavior problems in the traditional sense but their lack of social and academic skills can seriously handicap their classroom performance. When learning theory principles are used to build up or condition behaviors which are extremely weak, we speak of a prosthetic application since the treatment goal is to remediate a deficit in some area of functioning. Methods of strengthening a behavior include the use of differential reinforcement, social reinforcement, token reinforcement, and the Premack hypothesis. The following series of frames provide examples of how these techniques can be used in the classroom.

---

41. In prosthetic applications of learning theory, extensive use is made of the Premack hypothesis which states that high probability behaviors can be used to reinforce and thereby _____ low probability behaviors.

42. If running, jumping, and yelling are high probability behaviors for five-year-old kindergarten boys and sitting still, working quietly, and paying attention are low probability behaviors, then these high probability behaviors can be programmed to _____ and strengthen the low probability behaviors.

43. We could require, for example, that the boys produce twenty minutes of sitting still, working quietly, and paying attention in exchange for two minutes of running, jumping, and yelling in the gym. In this way, the _____ probability behaviors are being used to strengthen the _____ probability behaviors.

---

41. strengthen

42. reinforce

43. high
    low

81

44. As another example, suppose that a child detests reading—low probability—and is very interested and skilled in science—high probability. How could you use the Premack hypothesis most effectively?

_____a. require equal amounts of time spent in reading and working on science projects.

_____b. require small amounts of reading in exchange for large amounts of time spent in science.

_____c. require moderate to large amounts of reading in exchange for small amounts of time spent in science activities.

45. In conditioning very weak responses, it is necessary to _____ the learning situation so that competing or interfering responses are controlled.

46. It would be difficult to teach listening skills to a child in a chaotic and uncontrolled classroom setting. Before we could teach listening skills, we would have to gain ___control___ of the learning situation.

47. For learning to be effective, we have to eliminate conditions which suppress or _____ the desired behavior from occurring. One way of doing this is to structure the learning situation so there is a high probability that the desired response will be emitted and _____.

---

44. c

45. arrange, program, structure (or) set-up

46. control

47. prevent (or) preclude

reinforced, rewarded (or) strengthened

48. The process by which positive reinforcers are used to increase the probability that a behavior will occur again is known as _____ reinforcement.

49. In conditioning behavior, positive reinforcement is often used in a differential fashion. For example, if we wished to differentiate *one* response out of a large class of on-going responses, we would reinforce (all on-going responses, only the selected response) and withhold reinforcement from (all other responses, only the selected response).

50. If we reinforce each occurrence of a classroom behavior and withhold reinforcement whenever it does *not* occur, we are _____entially reinforcing that behavior.

51. In situation #50 reinforcement is _____ upon production of the desired response.

52. A contingency refers to the _____ between a response and a reinforcer.

53. If a specifiable, functional relationship exists between a reinforcer and a response, then reinforcement is said to be contingent. If there is no such relationship, then reinforcement is said to be _____-contingent.

---

48. positive

49. only the selected response
    all other responses

50. differ

51. dependent (or) contingent

52. arrangement (or) relationship

53. non (or) not

54. In many classrooms, the relationship between appropriate academic and social behaviors and reinforcement is non-contingent and the relationship between inappropriate academic and social behaviors and reinforcement is _____.

55. In this type of learning environment, the child learns that inappropriate social and academic behaviors—out-of-seat, talking out, creating classroom disruptions, not paying attention— produce _____ from the teacher in the form of negative attention—scolding, disapproval, warnings, etc. Appropriate social and academic behaviors—sitting still, working quietly, paying attention, completing assignments on time—do not produce reinforcement in the form of attention, praise, or approval.

56. The result of these contingency arrangements is that inappropriate behavior is (strengthened, weakened) and appropriate behavior is (strengthened, weakened).

57. To produce a constructive, efficient learning environment, the above contingency arrangements have to be _____.

58. Contingency arrangements in the classroom should be established so children learn that appropriate social/academic behavior is noticed and _____ positively while inappropriate social/academic behaviors are either ignored or weakened through punishment procedures.

---

54. contingent

55. reinforcement (or) reward

56. strengthened
    weakened

57. reversed (or) turned around

58. reinforced (or) rewarded

59. There are three types of positive _____ which the teacher can program and control in the classroom setting. These include: 1) nutrient, 2) abstract, and 3) social reinforcers. Nutrient reinforcers usually consist of candy or food. Abstract reinforcers include points, tokens, gold stars, or grades. Social reinforcers refer to expressions or gestures of praise, attention, interest, approval and affection.

60. Most classroom behavior can be controlled and regulated without the use of nutrient reinforcers (true, false).

61. Many effective classroom teachers make extensive use of _____ and _____ reinforcers.

62. There are many (extrinsic, intrinsic) reinforcers which operate naturally in the classroom environment to reinforce and maintain academic responses. These intrinsic reinforcers include mastery of a task, acquisition of new or interesting knowledge, task completion, positive feedback associated with making correct responses, etc. It would be very (easy, difficult) for the teacher to manipulate such intrinsic reinforcers directly.

63. There are a small number of children in the school setting who do not have the necessary skills to produce such _____ reinforcement for themselves. There are others who are not motivated to seek such reinforcement. There are also students for whom task mastery, task completion, and acquisition of new knowledge are simply not reinforcing. These children are

---

59. consequences, (or) reinforcers

60. true

61. abstract
    social

62. intrinsic
    difficult

85

often referred to as underachievers who have either learning or behavioral disorders. Such children usually require some form of _extrinsic_, positive reinforcement to build or to strengthen the required academic and social behaviors which contribute to success in school.

64. It is important to remember that all "problem" children do not respond to the same reinforcer(s). One child may prefer to work for small amounts of free time to engage in some favorite activity such as reading, art work, or science. With another child, systematic teacher attention and praise may be sufficient to maintain his attempts at appropriate, classroom behavior. With still another, it may be necessary to reinforce with tokens which can be exchanged for a model or toy. For an intervention program to be effective, the _____ must be appropriate for the child.

65. It is important that the child's classroom behavior be brought under the eventual control of _____so_____ reinforcers dispensed by his learning environment, i.e., teachers, peers, materials.

66. Social reinforcers, dispensed by the teacher, are occasionally neutral or even aversive stimuli for some children because of a long history of negative connotations associated with their dispensement—scolding, scowling, verbal abuse, warnings, frowns, etc. In these instances, the incentive value of teacher-dispensed social reinforcers can be enhanced systematically by pairing _____, social reinforcers with points, stars, or tokens which can be exchanged for back-up reinforcers such as free time, grades, or trinkets.

---

63. intrinsic
    external (or) extrinsic

64. reinforcer

65. social, intrinsic (or) natural

66. positive

67. Once the behavior has been conditioned and strengthened, tangible reinforcement—points, stars, tokens—can gradually be _____, leaving the behavior under the control of teacher-dispensed, social reinforcement.

67. withdrawn

SET 4: *Procedure for Modifying a Behavior*

The specific intervention program required for modifying a classroom behavior will usually vary according to the behavior being modified. However, there is a general set of procedures which can be followed in the process of modifying most classroom behaviors. The purpose of such behavior modification is to increase the rates of appropriate classroom behaviors and to decrease the rates of inappropriate classroom behaviors.

---

68. The first step usually involves a statement or isolation of the target behavior. The overt units of the behavior are specified and described. The procedure for ＿＿＿＿＿＿ the behavior is made—rate, duration, frequency.

69. The operant level of the behavior must be established next. The behavior is observed in order to get an estimate of its rate or ＿＿＿＿＿＿.

70. The observation data are analyzed. Reinforcing and/or aversive events which ＿＿＿＿＿＿ the behavior are pinpointed. Antecedent cues or stimuli which (precede, follow) the response are noted and functional relationships are specified.

---

68. monitoring, measuring (or)   70. maintain, control
    recording   precede

69. frequency

71. Environmental events or stimuli—reinforcers, materials, contingencies—that can be manipulated in order to _____ change _____ the behavior or change the response rate are specified.

72. The intervention program is planned and initiated. Observations are taken and the _____ effects _____ of the intervention program are evaluated.

---

71. modify   72. effects (or) results

SET 5: *Procedure for Shaping a Behavior*

As mentioned earlier in section A, shaping refers to a process in which a new response is built into the behavioral repertoire through the reinforcement of successive approximations to some terminal performance. The skill to be acquired is described in functional terms and broken down into components which are conditioned by gradually raising the criterion for reinforcement. Shaping is especially useful in the acquisition of complex skills which are not readily acquired through demonstration, trial and error, or rote learning.

---

73. Select the behavior or skill which is to be _____ and break it down into small, discrete units which can be arranged in a sequence.

74. Provide a learning situation in which competing responses are controlled and the probability (increased, decreased) that the desired response will be emitted. Structure the situation carefully, monitor the performance continuously, and provide positive feedback *and* cues for correct responses.

75. Select a _____ to which the child is responsive.

---

73. acquired

74. increased

75. reinforcer, reward (or) consequating event

76. Shape each discrete unit of the behavior separately and in the proper _____ sequence _____. Reinforce successive _____ approximations _____ to the final performance of each component in the sequence. Raise the criterion for _____ reinforcement _____ gradually. Make the reinforcement (immediate, delayed) and continuous for appropriate responses.

77. When all components in the sequence have been _____ achieved _____, link them together through a process called chaining. Only reinforce production of the complete response from this point on.

78. Gradually shift from a continuous to an _____ intermittent _____ schedule of reinforcement and fade out the tangible reinforcement.

79. Monitor the behavior as necessary and keep _____ records _____ on the number of times it is performed to criterion as determined by rate, frequency, or percentage correct.

---

76. sequence

    approximations

    reinforcement

    immediate

77. mastered, achieved (or) completed

78. intermittent

79. records, data, (or) charts

SUMMARY

1. Behavior change is an observable alteration in overt behavior.
2. Behavior technology has been found to be superior to traditional psychotherapy in producing behavior change.
3. The primary goal of therapeutic applications of learning theory is to weaken or "stamp out" deviant behavior.
4. In prosthetic applications, the primary goal is to build in or condition behaviors whose operant levels are low.
5. Behavior modification techniques are usually programmed to increase or decrease behavior rates.
6. Shaping is used to establish totally new responses in the individual's behavioral repertoire.

References

Allport, F. H. *Social psychology*. Cambridge, Mass.: Riverside Press, 1924.

Ayllon, T. Intensive treatment of psychotic behaviour by stimulus satiation and food reinforcement. In Ullman, L. P. and Krasner, L. (Eds.) *Case studies in behavior modification*. New York: Holt, Rinehart and Winston, 1966.

Bandura, A. and Walters, R. H. Aggression. In *Child psychology: The sixty-second yearbook of the National Society for the Study of Education* Part 1. Chicago: The National Society for the Study of Education, 1963, 364—415. (a)

Bandura, A. and Walters, R. H. *Social learning and personality development*. New York: Holt, Rinehart and Winston, 1963. (b)

Bandura, A., Ross, Dorothea, & Ross, Shiela A. Transmission of aggression through imitation of aggressive models. *Journal of Abnormal Social Psychology*, 1961, *63*, 575—582.

Bandura, A., Ross, Dorothea, & Ross, Shiela A. Imitation of film-mediated aggressive models. *Journal of Abnormal Social Psychology*, 1963, *66*, 3—11.

Bijou, S. W. Experimental studies of child behavior, normal and deviant. In Krasner, L. and Ullman, L. P. (Eds.) *Research in behavior modification*. New York: Holt, Rinehart and Winston, 1966.

Bijou, S. W., Birnbrauer, J. S., Kidder, J. D. and Tague, C. Programmed instruction as an approach to teaching of reading, writing and arithmetic to retarded children. In S. W. Bijou & D. M. Baer (Eds.) *Child development: Readings in experimental analysis*. New York: Appleton-Century-Crofts, 1967.

Becker, W. C., Madsen, C. H., Jr., Arnold, Carole R., and Thomas, D. R. The contingent use of teacher attention and praise in reducing classroom behavior problems. *Journal of Special Education*, 1967, *1*, 287—307.

Butler, R. A. Discrimination learning by rhesus monkeys to visual-exploration motivation. *The Journal of Comparative and Physiological Psychology*, 1953, *46*, 95—98.

Butler, R. A. & Alexander, H. M. Daily patterns of visual exploratory behavior in the monkey. *The Journal of Comparative and Physiological Psychology*, 1955, *48*, 247—249.

Estes, K. W. An experimental study of punishment. *Psychological Monographs*, 1944, *57*(263), 40.

Eysenck, H. J. The effects of psychotherapy. *Journal of Consulting Psychology*, 1952, *16*, 319—324.

Eysenck, H. J. The effects of psychotherapy. In *Handbook of Abnormal Psychology*. London: Pitman, 1960.

Gaasholt, Marie. University of Oregon. Personal communication, 1969.

Hall, R. V., Lund, Diane and Jackson, Deloris. Effects of teacher attention on study behavior. *Journal of Applied Behavior Analysis*, 1968, *1*, 1—12.

Hilgard, E. R. *Introduction to psychology*. (3rd ed.) New York: Harcourt, 1962.

Humphrey, G. Imitation and the conditioned reflex. *Pedagogical Seminary Journal of Genetic Psychology*, 1921, *28*, 1—21.

Kuypers, D. S., Becker, W. C. and O'Leary, K. D. How to make a token economy fail. *Exceptional Children*, 1968, *35*(2), 101—109.

Landau, R. & Gewirtz, J. L. Differential satiation for a social reinforcing stimulus as a determinant of its efficacy in conditioning. *Journal of Experimental Child Psychology*, 1967, *5*, 391—405.

Levitt, E. E. The results of psychotherapy with children. *Journal of Consulting Psychology*, 1957, *21*, 189—195.

Levitt, E. E. Psychotherapy with children. A further evaluation. *Behaviour Research and Therapy*, 1963, *1*, 45—51.

Lohr, T. F. The effect of shock on the rat's choice of a path to food. *Journal of Experimental Psychology*, 1959, *58*, 312—318.

McClelland, D. C. *Personality*. New York: William Sloane Associates, 1951.

Mechner, F. A notation system for the description of behavioral procedures. *Journal of the Experimental Analysis of Behavior*, 1959, *2*, 133—150.

Miller, N. E. and Dollard, J. *Social learning and imitation*. New Haven: Yale University Press, 1941.

Morse, W. H. Intermittent reinforcement. In Honig, W. K. (Ed.) *Operant behavior: Areas of research and application*. New York: Appleton-Century-Crofts, 1966.

Mowrer, O. H. *Learning theory and the symbolic processes*. New York: Wiley, 1960.

Murray, E. J. *Motivation and Emotion*. New Jersey: Prentice-Hall, 1964.

Piaget, J. *The child's conception of the world*. New York: Harcourt, Brace and World, 1929.

Skinner, B. F. *Science and human behavior*. New York: Macmillan, 1953.

Skinner, B. F. *The technology of teaching*. New York: Appleton-Century-Crofts, 1968.

Thomas, D. R., Becker, W. C. & Armstrong, M. Production and elimination of disruptive classroom behavior by systematically varying teacher's behavior. *Journal of Applied Behavior Analysis*, 1968, *1*, 35—45.

Tyler, V. O., Jr. & Brown, G. D. The use of swift, brief isolation as a group control device for institutionalized delinquents. *Behaviour Research and Therapy*, 1967, *5*, 1—9.

Walker, H. M., Mattson, R. H. and Buckley, Nancy K. Special class placement as a treatment alternative for deviant behavior in children. In F. A. M. Benson (Ed.) *Modifying deviant social behaviors in various classroom settings*. Eugene, Ore.: Dept. of Spec. Ed. Mono. #1. U. of O.

Walker, H. M. and Buckley, Nancy K. The use of positive reinforcement in conditioning attending behavior. *Journal of Applied Behavior Analysis*, 1968, *1*, 245—250.

Wolf, M., Risley, T. and Mees, H. Application of operant conditioning procedures to the behaviour problems of an autistic child. *Behaviour Research and Therapy*, 1964, *1*, 305—312.

Zimmerman, Elaine H. and Zimmerman, J. The alteration of behavior in a special classroom situation. In Ulrich, R., Stachnik, T. and Mabry, J. (Eds.) *Control of Human Behavior*, Illinois: Scott, Foresman & Co., 1966.

List of Suggested Readings

1. Benson, F. A. M. (Ed.) *Modifying deviant social behaviors in various classroom settings.* Department of Special Education, University of Oregon, 1969, No. 1.
2. Homme, L., Csanyi, A., Gonzales, M. and Rechs, J. *How to use contingency contracting in the classroom.* Illinois: Research Press, 1968.
3. Millenson, J. R. *Principles of behavioral analysis.* New York: Macmillan, 1968.
4. Patterson, G. R. and Gullion, M. Elizabeth. *Living with children: New methods for parents and teachers.* Illinois: Research Press, 1968.
5. Skinner, B. F. *The technology of teaching.* New York: Appleton-Century-Crofts, 1968.
6. Ullman, L. P. and Krasner, L. (Eds.) *Case studies in behavior modification.* New York: Holt, Rinehart and Winston, Inc., 1966.